BEYOND THE CLASSROOM:
Black Male Educators Changing the Narrative

Contributing Authors: David André Bennett, Ernest Clinkscale, Joel V. Coppadge II, Fredrick King, Jay Manning, Steven D. Mills, Scott Reeves, Tyler Rutledge & Michael J. Warren, Ed.D.

Foreword by: Michael R. Bean Jr., Ph.D.

Compiled by: Garrett M. Carter, Ph.D.

This book is dedicated to Black male educators who are impacting students' lives, shaping communities, and changing the narrative.

Table of Contents

Chapter 1...1

Chapter 2..11

Chapter 3..23

Chapter 4..35

Chapter 5..45

Chapter 6..55

Chapter 7..67

Chapter 8..77

Chapter 9..87

Chapter 10..99

Final Word...109

Foreword by Michael R. Bean Jr., Ph.D.

I have always believed in the transformative power of education. From my days as a student-athlete at Hampton University to my current role as Associate Professor, Director of Diversity, Equity, and Inclusion, and Assistant Women's Basketball Coach at Concord University, my journey has been marked by a relentless pursuit of improving educational outcomes for all students.

During my career as a K-12 teacher and administrator, I further developed my leadership skills realizing the systemic change that I could facilitate. While serving as a principal, my school surpassed local district benchmarks on state testing earning recognition from the Ohio Department of Education with a prestigious Momentum Award.

Throughout my career, I have remained steadfast in my belief that every student, regardless of their background or circumstances, is capable of learning and achieving success. My dedication has been recognized through numerous accolades and awards, all of which underscore my commitment to putting "Learners First and Foremost in Every Decision."

My journey from student-athlete to influential educator is a testament to the profound impact one person can have on the field of education. My innovative approach and unwavering dedication have not only transformed schools but have also inspired a new generation of educational leaders to strive for excellence and equity in every aspect of their work. The contributors featured in this work –all Black males in a variety of educational roles– are passionate educators with powerful stories to share. They, too, are partners in this important work.

As an educator, one of my proudest achievements is the impact that I have had on my students. The heartfelt moments, when former students return to express how I influenced their lives, deeply resonate with me. Many of my former students have gone on to achieve remarkable success by becoming pastors, doctors, lawyers, firefighters, and educators. Their achievements are a testament to my life's work and highlight the essential role that Black male educators play not only in our educational system but in our society at large. As you encounter eye-opening and inspiring stories in this book, I hope you will gain a new understanding of the transformative power of education along with a new appreciation for Black male educators committed to doing this important work.

Introduction by Garrett M. Carter, Ph.D.

The purpose of this book is to highlight the perspectives, experiences, and insights of Black male educators whose numbers are small but whose impact is mighty. Specifically, this book features nine Black male educators who have held various positions within the K-12 education system allowing for a broad yet intimate look at their journeys. At the end of each chapter, a summary captures key ideas presented by the contributing authors. Additionally, there are reflection pages for readers to interact with these stories and reflect upon their educational experiences.

While many will benefit from reading this book, there are two primary audiences in mind. First, these stories will undoubtedly resonate with Black male educators (past, present, and future). If you are a Black male educator reading this book, you may be the only individual in your building who looks like you. As you read these stories, the authors hope you find validation in the fact that you are not alone in the important work that you do daily. Second, the hope is that these stories will inform readers of all colors about the experiences of Black male educators so that there is a better understanding of the struggles, triumphs, and impact of these men. With an enhanced understanding, the authors hope that better support networks can be built within the educational system that will ultimately assist with the recruitment and retention efforts of Black male educators.

This book is organized into 10 chapters each based on a central question, with the educators/ contributing authors responding. As you read these powerful stories, visualize this work as a Q&A featuring an interviewer sitting in a circle with nine fellow Black male educators to explore their experiences in a safe space.

Now, picture these individuals in the middle of a large room with picture frames covering the walls. Within these frames are various people and places. Some of these photographs are black and white and a bit blurry while others are colorful and clear. Some of the photographs feature ancestors and mentors who played pivotal roles in these educators' lives and others are the students, families, and schools whose existence has both influenced and been influenced by these men. As you take in this image, you realize that there are too many pictures to count, and you are struck by the immeasurable impact of these educators. Indeed, this imagery inspired the creation of this book's title, *Beyond the Classroom: Black Male Educators Changing the Narrative.*

BEYOND THE CLASSROOM:

Black Male Educators Changing the Narrative

Chapter 1

Question: First, describe the path(s) leading you into the field of education.

David: I count it a blessing to have been taught and influenced by some of the finest educators. Because teachers were highly revered in my family and in my faith community, I would play school with my cousins. They, describing me as bossy and wanting to be in charge, would designate me as the teacher. I loved having the opportunity to mimic teachers that I admired. This love continued as I was constantly exposed to music-making. My family, especially my Uncle Samuel Bennett, a college music professor, my middle and high school choral directors; Mrs. Deborah Williamson and Mrs. Rosemary Renshler, and church choir directors all helped to foster my interest in music. Even though I initially entered college as a pre-med major, I later followed my passion for music. After seven years of teaching music and seeing the large disparities in the school system for African American children including not enough Black men in positions of influence, I realized that I could make a difference on a larger scale and decided to pursue educational leadership.

Ernest: Growing up in Youngstown, Ohio, my parents always stressed to my sister and me that education was the path to ultimate success. My mother worked as a teacher's aide in the GED program. When I would visit her, I was always taken aback at the concept of adults not being able to read and write. I knew that I wanted to do something about that when I got older so going into education was always my focus from a young age. When I was in high school, I knew that I wanted to go to college, and I knew that I wanted to teach. I originally committed to Kent State University due to its strong education program but ended up attending Ohio University just like my older sister.

Fredrick: I graduated with my degree in psychology because I wanted to contribute to society by helping youth develop skills to live healthy independent lives. I began my career working as a skills development specialist at an agency that provides services to foster care and at-risk youth in the community. I was responsible for teaching my clients strategies to overcome barriers within their lives as well as develop skills to live successfully on their own once they aged out of the foster care system. My position provided me with a unique opportunity to get a small glimpse of what life was like for youth in the foster care system. I noticed that many of my clients in foster care went from several different placements or living situations within short periods of time. Since foster care placements were limited, many of my clients were placed in new foster homes far from their base schools and had to re-enroll in another school. I remember attending school meetings for my clients and noticing that many of them were falling significantly behind academically due to having to start over at a different school. It often appeared that this concern of mine was not shared with other school team members in the room. In these moments, I felt my clients needed someone to advocate on their behalf. This realization was ultimately the catalyst that catapulted me into considering the field of education in order to advocate for marginalized youth.

Jay: Born into a family full of servicemen and educators, I was exposed to the dynamics of education and discipline early on in my youth. I soon realized that I also shared a passion for educating our youth and empowering them to be the best versions of themselves. It was not until after my semi-professional basketball career ended that I learned that God's plan for me did not involve joining the brotherhood of the National Basketball Association (NBA), but instead involved joining the fraternity of education to impact the next generation. During my undergraduate and graduate years of college, I majored in middle grades education, curriculum and instruction, and participated in administrative internships where I gained valuable field experience at various schools. Upon earning a bachelor's degree in education with a minor in biblical studies, I accepted a teaching and head basketball coaching position in Lagrange, Georgia, and started my educational career. I have not looked back since, and currently serve as a high school assistant principal.

Tyler: My initial career was not education; it was as a military medic. I believed that I could make a change in the world by utilizing the military to go through the medical field and be of service to the people around me. As I moved back into the civilian world and entered nursing school, I had a desire to become a nursing teacher in hopes that my influence could be further reached. Due to a few challenges with mental health which correlated with the medical profession, I decided it was not a fit for me. As such, I followed a love that I had put on hold and pursued education. I knew that if I could make a difference in the life of just one student throughout my entire career, then I would be a success.

Scott: When I stepped onto the campus of Ohio State University as a freshman in the fall of 1987, I had no idea what profession to choose. Despite their honest intentions, my parents did not know how to help me. Early in my sophomore year, with the impending decision of selecting an academic major looming on the horizon, fate guided me to my former high school. One day, for some unusual reason, my parents asked me to bring my younger sister home from school. I arrived at Eastmoor High School early enough to visit my favorite teachers and coaches. Strolling down the hallways wrapped in my scarlet Varsity O letter jacket, I soaked in the adulation of my teachers, each of whom smiled at me with genuine pride. And that was it. High school, I realized, gave me a lifetime of memories and positive experiences. The environment drew me in, and within weeks of my high school visit, I entered the Ohio State College of Education. History fascinated me because of the stories my grandmother, born in 1894, entertained me with as a child. Her elegant tales transported me back to the time of the great trains and horse carriages. I relished graduating in 1992 with a degree in Social Studies Education - just two months shy of my grandmother's passing. She was very proud.

Joel: The path that led me to the field of education was my desire to help other people. My first taste of that desire was serving as a math tutor while a student at Morehouse College. Growing up I would hear people, whether it was adults, classmates, or even my relatives, that declared math was not for them. Yet, learning mathematics was natural for me. It was the perfect way to use my understanding to help my fellow collegiate classmates learn basic math. I continued tutoring after college before becoming a teacher. However, it was during the many tutoring sessions that I learned patience. It was here that I tailored instruction to the needs of the student and became aware that not every student learns the same way. More importantly, I realized that my desire to help other people learn math continued to grow.

Michael: By the year 2011, I had been in six foster homes, adopted, become a ward of the court due to a failed adoption, and reentered the foster care system. Education was a way for me to escape the harsh realities of what I considered to be a dismal life. Though I grew to love school, it was often challenging to find the benefits of education for a little Black boy out of the hood when I was regularly met with teachers who did not believe in me or an educational system that showed no promise for a life better than what I was currently experiencing. That was until I entered middle school. The start of my middle school journey was rocky. However, by the time I was transitioning to high school, I began to believe that I was worth something and that my life had meaning. I attended a performing arts middle school and was exposed to travel, culture, and students from various backgrounds. Here, I also experienced my first

Black male teacher. Fast forward nearly 10 years later, and I dropped out of college twice. I had cancer, kidney failure, and experienced homelessness due to lack of income. Still, I was determined to overcome the many obstacles life had presented me and accomplish my dreams. I went on to complete my bachelor's in music education, my master's in education, and a doctorate in educational leadership. No matter the educational journey I took to get to where I am, my mission remains the same: to serve as an inspiration for other students like my middle school chorus teacher, Mr. Henry Biggs, was for me. He truly changed my life forever.

Steven: My fight for literacy paved my path to education. I hated school. Growing up, I did not feel the love and support I needed to thrive. The schools did not consider the whole child, just my negative and impulsive behavior, uncleanliness, or the fact that I had two uneducated, uninvolved, and sometimes negligent parents. I felt judged and misunderstood. I was held back in the second grade and earned straight Fs in the seventh grade. I read at a second-grade level until middle school. When I met the adults who would later become my legal guardians, they realized I needed love, guidance, and most of all, glasses. After one year of tutoring and corrective lenses, my reading comprehension improved dramatically. That is when my hatred for school turned into a desire to change what I viewed as a broken system for young students like me. After serving as a substitute teacher, I realized that my genuine desire was to teach, model, and shape elementary minds. I enrolled at Central State so that I could complete my degree in early childhood education.

Summary

While each educator's pathway varied, one significant commonality was the idea of being of service to others. Indeed, educators have opportunities to change lives in ways that are impossible to measure. Pouring into students, who then take those life lessons and pour into others, is not only gratifying but it is one way that communities can improve over time. In addition to wanting to serve others, another idea that emerged was that several of these men had someone supporting, mentoring, and believing in them early on in life which helped them to overcome various obstacles or otherwise guide them to their journey as an educator. Michael, for instance, credits his teacher and mentor with changing his life. Now, as educators themselves, the authors are positioned to serve as mentors for others on a much larger scale.

Chapter 1 Reflection

Record your thoughts, notes, and takeaways below.

_____

_____

_____

_____

_____

_____

_____

_____

_____

_____

_____

_____

_____

_____

Chapter 2

Question: What type of school setting(s) have you worked in, and how has your identity as a Black male shaped your experiences?

David: As a music educator and administrator at the elementary and high school levels, I have served in both urban and suburban settings. The urban settings consisted of inner-city schools, whose student populations were mostly African American, or from students from Appalachian Regions. These students were disproportionately from low-income and predominantly single-parent homes, and all of these schools were designated as Title I buildings. Alternately, the suburban settings were predominantly upper-middle-class, affluent Caucasian children.

Students' self-esteem, sense of worth, and hope for their future are enhanced when they see themselves represented in leadership positions. Thus, Black children need to have teachers and administrators of color. Many African American teachers tend to view children of color as their own, while still holding them accountable to higher expectations. These educators know firsthand the obstacles students are likely to face and have a strong desire to ensure that they are equipped to meet them. Black students need to see teachers who look like them and ones that can relate to their personal experiences. Educators can pull sources, make references, and provide relevant examples to which students can connect. Then, students are more likely to understand complex concepts, thoughts, and ideas. Having representation helps students develop resilience, self-esteem, and the capacity to see beyond the present. Black educators become great advocates for students and serve as cheerleaders of their success both in and out of the classroom.

Ernest: I have worked in both large urban districts and suburban districts in many different roles. I have worked as a teacher, math specialist, and administrator. Many times, I have been the only Black male in the entire building so that always shaped my experience. I was often given the task of working with the students that the building viewed as "challenging." This would often consist of Black male students. In my role as an administrator in a suburban district, I oftentimes have worked as a go-to for many of my parents of color who only feel comfortable having me deal with them and their kids.

Fredrick: I have worked as a school psychologist both at the primary and secondary levels. Within these settings, I noticed that there were not many Black male educators in the building, particularly while working at my elementary school. I became hyperaware of my identity as a Black man and felt the responsibility to be a visible figure to my students, especially to my Black students. I needed to communicate to Black students that there was someone in the building who they could connect with and relate to from a cultural standpoint. I took extra time in my day to visit the lunchroom, playground, and walk the hallways to interact with my students and to introduce myself to them. Since I did not have any Black male teachers during my entire school career, I wanted to ensure that my Black students had someone who they could feel safe around.

Jay: I have worked in lower-income, Title I public school settings and suburban public school settings. In the lower-income schools, I often worked with students who experienced a lack of parental support, free or reduced lunch, gang-related activities, and/or average to below-average test scores. As a Black male in this setting, I found that I was relatable for most minority students and that I instantly found myself wearing many "hats" including teacher, mentor, and father figure. As a Black male in the suburban school setting, I found that some parents had lower expectations of me. I realized that certain students, staff, and parents did not understand or empathize with African American or minority culture. In summary, being a Black male has both positively and negatively shaped my experiences in school settings. However, I fully embrace being a Black male educator and aim to empower others to do the same.

Tyler: Thus far, my educational career has been in a large suburban district. Within my school, there is a higher rate of diversity which played a large role in my decision to take this position. Being a Black male guided me to this setting because of my desire for students of color to experience a teacher who looks like them. Within my school, there is a small contingent of teachers of color, but within the district, we have an organization in which all educators of color connect as a community to fellowship and discuss our experiences. This provides me with an affirmational experience that I have never had previously. Through family, I have had connections to my culture and history, but connecting with other educators of color has provided me an opportunity to express myself in a way that I cannot fully express with my other colleagues.

Scott: My identity as a Black male and my tight circle of comfort regarding the demographics of a school where I would want to teach was the sole influence at the start of my teaching career. As a graduate of an urban school system, an environment of rich diversity defined my entire experience as a student. Although my classmates were a healthy representation of different cultures, religions, and races, my closest group of friends were Black. Likewise, in my journey through a predominantly white university, my friends were primarily Black. After graduating from college, I had two options for my first teaching job. The first came from the school district from where I graduated. That district offered me a teaching contract, although they did not have an available teaching position. The other offer came from an adjoining suburb that recently opened a new high school. I toured the impressive new building and fielded calls from Black parents imploring me to accept a job in the new school. I chose the comfort of my home district.

After teaching there for nearly a decade, I became an administrator in a rapidly diversifying but still predominantly white suburb. The principal of that suburban school was none other than my high school principal from my days as a student. As a highly respected Black male educator, he helped me to significantly expand my circle of comfort. Since transitioning to the suburbs as an assistant principal, I have been a high school principal, held various district administrative positions, and am currently an assistant superintendent in another diverse suburban district. Now 30 years into my career, serving in a racially homogeneous school district still has no appeal to me. I relish my experiences with the spectrum of families –Black and white, Muslim and Christian, domestic and international– that I've enjoyed in communities beyond the comfort of home.

Joel: The school settings that I have worked in include both public and charter schools. Both avenues have helped shape my experience as a Black male by providing me with different perspectives from fellow teachers, students, and staff. This includes understanding different school environments, cultures, and ways of life.

Michael: Upon graduating from college, I was determined to work in the inner city because I was a product of urban education. I had experiences that allowed me to relate to some of the challenges students in an urban setting would face, and I believed my path to education could be a motivating factor for students who came from a similar background as me. Leading up to graduation, I signed on to become a long-term sub in an urban setting. I learned that even with my experiences as a student in the inner city, there was a clear gap in terms of the way pre-service teachers were prepared to serve students in non-suburban settings. I felt unprepared and felt that I was not cut out for this field.

My time in the suburban setting was truly shocking and fulfilling at the same time. Never did I believe I could have an impact on students who did not look like me, which is why I struggled to accept my transition from teaching in an urban school to teaching in a suburban school. Additionally, it was one thing to feel bad for leaving the city setting, but to be called a "sell-out" by colleagues for "leaving" Black and Brown kids was a hard pill to swallow. During my first year as a teacher in the suburbs, I met a student whose parents were going through a divorce, causing this student to act out in class. One day during his lunch detention, we began to talk about his family and interests, and I began to ask how I could support him. I remember telling him he could join his classmates and he said he would rather stay and continue talking. This resulted in an "aha moment" for me. He just wanted someone to notice him and show that he was cared for. It was at this moment that I learned Black or white, suburban, rural, or urban, all kids deserve an educator who believes in them. Since this time, I have served as an administrator in both an urban PreK-8 building and a suburban PreK-5 building.

Steven: I did not have a male teacher until fourth grade, and I did not have a single Black teacher until fifth grade. For the first two years of my career, I served as a kindergarten teacher. I was warned early in my career that I would be moved out of the classroom quickly because I am a Black man. This prophecy became a reality when I took a position at the same school as a reading curriculum coach just two years later. I missed the classroom and disliked the curriculum position, so as soon as a teacher in my building took a leave of absence, I jumped at the opportunity to teach his first-grade class for the remainder of the year.

After that school year, I transitioned from my urban district to a suburban district and flourished under the amazing leadership of D.T. I did not want to leave my school district because I felt like I was betraying my culture by teaching in another district with less than 30% Black students. I shared my apprehension with my mentor and his statement will forever be etched in my memory. He said that there were many Black students in my new district who did not have an advocate or role model who looked like them. Further, he shared that there were a lot of white students who needed Black role models because all they know about Black people is what they see in the media or on social media.

Summary

Collectively, these educators have worked in urban and suburban settings shaping the learning and lives of students from all backgrounds. While these men are educators, they are Black male educators, and their identities are at the forefront of their consciousness and the work they do. The authors note the importance of students having a teacher or role model who looks like them, as many did not encounter a Black teacher in their own schooling. Being a Black male educator – sometimes the only one in the school– comes with a sense of responsibility and sometimes taking on additional roles both formal and informal. Multiple authors expressed experiencing some hesitancy or guilt by transitioning from a school that was predominately Black to a more racially diverse environment. However, as Steven's mentor shared with him, Black students exist in the suburbs and need support in these spaces too. Further, all students need to see Black males in teaching and leadership positions.

"I became hyperaware of my identity as a Black man and felt the responsibility to be a visible figure to my students, especially to my Black students. I needed to communicate to Black students that there was someone in the building who they could connect with and relate to from a cultural standpoint."

-Fredrick

Chapter 2 Reflection

Record your thoughts, notes, and takeaways below.

_____

_____

_____

_____

_____

_____

_____

_____

_____

_____

_____

_____

_____

Chapter 3
Question: What challenges or barriers have you faced as a Black male educator?

David: In my twenty-plus years as a Black male educator, I have been fortunate to work with some of the most talented, gifted, and caring administrators, educators, students, and families. Yet, challenges and barriers have been commonplace. I have often been misunderstood, misquoted, lied on, approached with conscious and unconscious bias, and disrespected. This has occurred in concert with me carrying the weight of being expected to speak on behalf of all Black students, parents, and the entire African American race. Many times, parents have questioned my decisions and my authority, though I followed district guidelines and regulations. They bypassed me to speak with my superiors regarding building policies, expectations, and protocols. I have experienced colleagues who have misquoted me and sometimes outright lied to bring my qualifications into question. As a Black male administrator, I have been excluded from "inner room" decision-making conversations that would directly impact my students, staff, and community. I have had the experience of being invited to a meeting with the superintendent and a parent to discuss a concern. Once I arrived, I unexpectedly found four parents which left me blindsided as the dynamics of this meeting had changed. The unsubstantiated criticism and blatant racism I have faced as an African American male educator from some parents, students, colleagues, and community members has caused me to ask, "Is it worth my investment?" "Can I expect a return?" and more importantly, "Am I making a difference?"

Ernest: It is hard to explain what it feels like to go into a building day after day where nobody or very few people look like you. It is often a feeling of loneliness and isolation. I have oftentimes seen my peers ascend to jobs and positions that I felt I was qualified for but was never given that opportunity. I am a person with three college degrees, including two master's degrees, but some people will only view me as a disciplinarian and not as an intellectual. Even though I have been in this career for 25 years, I still come into my school every day with the attitude that I must be perfect and outwork everyone just to prove that I deserve this job. Many of my peers do not have that pressure.

Fredrick: I am fortunate to not have experienced overt racism as a Black school psychologist, likely because my school district is more racially, culturally, and linguistically diverse than others. However, I have felt the burden of having to be more cautious of how I present myself to my

24

colleagues as a Black male. While this issue may be self-imposed, my awareness of the biases and stereotypes people typically hold of Black men adds extra pressure for me in my position to be an exceptional school psychologist. I have felt the need to be overly prepared to prove to others that I am great at my job and to prevent confirming people's stereotypes that they may have of Black men. Additionally, I have had to be very mindful of how I interact with my colleagues during various situations to ensure I do not come off as aggressive. While I recognize this is more of a societal issue than my own, the reality is that many Black men in traditionally white spaces tend to feel added pressures to prove their worth and may work to dispel negative stereotypes people hold. This has caused me to experience anxiety in situations where I felt I had to perform during school meetings to show my colleagues that I am the mental health expert in the room.

Jay: Although I do not believe in making excuses, I can acknowledge the fact that being a Black male educator creates more challenges and barriers for us. Among the many challenges and barriers that Black male educators endure, the main ones that I have faced include prejudice, lack of diversity and representation, microaggressions, and inadequate support. I have personally experienced being in a position of leadership and not receiving support or any feedback from white teachers when administering testing training for them. I have worked in environments with a lack of diversity among staff and witnessed microaggressions where white teachers exposed stereotypical thinking and made insensitive comments regarding Black culture. I have experienced some prejudice from staff who felt that I was incapable of completing the duties required of me as a leader, grade-level chair, and administrator due to age, gender, and race. Still, I consider myself blessed to serve as an administrator because of the lack of diversity and representation within school leadership positions and opportunities. With the percentage of Black male educators estimated to be in the low single digits in terms of the teacher workforce, we face challenges when it comes to finding mentors, role models, and networks.

Tyler: As a Black male teacher, I have faced more implicit barriers when it comes to fighting for change. As a teacher, I work diligently towards creating a more equitable environment for my students. However, I can only reach a small number of students each year. As I have joined different committees, I struggle with this concept as I try to increase the equitable components of the school. The bureaucracy has limited progress and prevented a more "radical" change. I have also faced times when my ideas were shut down, only to be submitted by a non-Black teacher and then they were accepted. Although not explicitly denying my voice, it was something that frustrated me and almost drove me away from continuing the fight for change.

Scott: In retrospect, I sensed minimal barriers as a Black male teacher in an urban school district. My district and building leaders were mostly Black, our school's student population was 90% Black, and we had several Black male and female staff members. On the contrary, I felt that doors opened for me rather than barriers placed in my path. Districts competed for Black male educators because there existed so few in the profession to model for and mentor Black students. Today, there are even fewer. As I prepared for my administration position in a nearby majority-white suburb, my Black colleagues cautioned me that the school would pigeonhole me with Black student issues and that the suburbs would never allow me to lead a building. Neither of those warnings became my reality. However, I did carry self-imposed anxiety into that suburb regarding how the white staff and community would receive me. Both were wonderful. The same would be true in my experience as a principal and a district leader. However, because the number of

Black male educators is so few, I lack a cohort of Black colleagues on whom I can lean for support and guidance. At an event with a hundred administrators, it would not be unusual for me to be either the only Black male in the room or one of a few. At a community event, even though my current suburban school district is statistically 50% students of color and 50% white, it is not unusual for me to be the only or one of just a few Black males in attendance. In the state's most populated county, excluding the large urban school district where Black male and female educators are numerically dominant, I am the highest-ranking Black male educator as an assistant superintendent among the county's 15 suburban districts. So, are there barriers? Certainly. I also know I likely faced obstacles covertly placed before me along the way. I am not naive to believe there were not.

Joel: The main challenges I have faced as a Black male educator have been being one of the few Black male educators in my school and being the youngest teacher amongst the middle school grades. I am currently in my second year as a math teacher, so my classroom experience is not as vast as some of my colleagues. To combat these challenges, I accept that I do not know everything about how to run a classroom and rely on my colleagues to help me with areas I may not understand. Whether it is to understand how to structure my grade book or keep my students on task, I have learned to accept help to better myself as a Black educator.

Michael: Coming out of college into my substitute teaching position, I faced a host of challenges in the inner city. However, those challenges I attribute to limited teaching experience, lack of classroom management skills, and inheriting a program with two months left of school. It was during my time teaching in the suburbs that I got my first reality check of being a Black male educator. It was as if this reminder was coming from students, parents, and other professionals in the field. The challenge of not being heard, having all my decisions questioned, and the host of microaggressions faced daily made teaching extremely difficult at times.

Working as an administrator in a suburban elementary setting, the intersectionality of being Black and male (and young) often plays a part in some of the challenges. My delivery has been interpreted as using a hostile tone, and I have even been told that my physical stature is scary and intimidating, making it hard for teachers to approach me. Trying to implement or even carry out initiatives seems impossible at times when facing these sorts of barriers. Another challenge of being a Black male educator is the expectation that I handle discipline for all students of color. I witnessed this a lot during my time in the urban schools. On one hand, with assumed positive intentions, it suggests colleagues feel that I can make connections with students of color. At the same time, it has often diminished the other educational value brought to the field due to the primary role of being a disciplinarian.

Steven: "He's arrogant, he's cocky, and he thinks he knows everything!" These were some of the things my principal told me that teachers were saying about me after my first year of teaching. I learned that their opinions had nothing to do with me. The same comments were made about several other strong Black educators I knew, some that I consider mentors. In those men, I see confidence, brilliance, and a passion to make a difference.

As a Black man, I am considered the disciplinary figure. Year after year, all the "challenging" Black students were placed in my class. I always felt like my class was a dumping ground. While in my mind, my role was to save every child, it burned me out. During my time teaching second grade, the team was made up of five middle-aged white women and me. In a school district that was roughly 30% minority, my classroom was 90% Black students. Most of them were Black boys who had issues in first grade and needed a strong male role model who looked like them. However, placing 10 students with behavior issues in the same classroom was overwhelming in every sense. It was an obvious problem. I distinctly remember an intervention specialist pointing it out as she walked into my classroom. It was noticed.

Summary

Because there are so few Black male educators, the authors have faced challenges and pressures that other educators do not experience. There is a sense of loneliness at times and also the pressure to excel because these men are not only representing themselves, but they are working hard to showcase the powerful impact that Black male educators bring to educational spaces. In other words, because they may be the only one in their building who looks like them, they know they are being watched and judged differently. Indeed, Ernest discusses the need to be perfect and outwork others while Fredrick speaks of his desire to defy stereotypes. Not only do these educators have their own job responsibilities to fulfill, but they often take on the role of disciplinarian for Black students that other teachers may have challenges with. Further, Black male educators must navigate all of this as they face microaggressions, have their qualifications and decisions questioned and, at times, are expected to speak on behalf of their entire race. Unsurprisingly, this has resulted in some of the authors feeling overwhelmed, dealing with anxiety, and questioning their efforts. However, despite these challenges, the authors remain committed to doing this important work.

Chapter 3 Reflection

Record your thoughts, notes, and takeaways below.

_____

_____

_____

_____

_____

_____

_____

_____

_____

_____

_____

_____

_____

Chapter 4

Question: My dissertation* cites scholars who find numerous academic and social-emotional benefits that Black educators have on Black students (along with students of other races). Based on your experiences, why does this occur?

David: Students want teachers who respect and believe in them. Their existence and worth need validation. Students desire teachers who see them, hear them, embrace their diversity, and have the ability to connect to them in meaningful and powerful ways. Black students flourish when given the golden opportunity to teach others and share their unique stories and ideas. Black educators are more inclined to invest the time and exert the effort required to create safe spaces where students feel comfortable opening up, asking questions, and speaking their truth. Students of color need to see and connect with role models who look like them and can relate to their cultural experiences. Once trust has been established and students know a teacher genuinely cares for them, they will work extremely hard to meet and often exceed expectations. Black educators have sat where Black students are now sitting and they understand the challenges they face. The influence of Black educators is monumental in setting high expectations, motivating students toward their full potential, and being fully committed to students' personal, academic, and overall life success.

Ernest: One cannot assume that just because a person of color is placed in front of students of color that somehow guarantees success. Oftentimes, Black male educators are successful because we are emotionally invested and understand what a difference an education can make for our young people. I also knew it was important for me to show my young men of color that there was another path to success that you could take that did not involve a football or a basketball. I wore a shirt and tie every day and carried a briefcase. I needed my young people of color to see that they too could use their minds to be successful in life.

Fredrick: During my time as a student, I only had two Black teachers from preschool through grad school. I remember not being fully aware of my racial identity in early childhood until my white counterparts began to make more and more racially driven remarks about my skin, hair, clothes, and vernacular. When I raised some of these concerns to my white teachers, they typically did not know how to appropriately respond to the situation due to their lack of understanding of how these remarks may impact students of color. I remember experiencing prejudice many times while at school and feeling as though I had no one to turn to who would understand or adequately address these issues with my white peers. Since there were not many educators in the building who looked like me, I often felt isolated and misunderstood. Further, I did not feel advocated for or represented within the educational curriculum. Therefore, representation of Black educators within schools is essential to ensuring that all students feel a sense of safety and belonging. Without Black educators, many students of color may suffer in silence if they do not feel they have someone willing to speak on their behalf. Black educators provide a unique perspective and voice to educational decisions impacting students and, without them, these insights would be overlooked.

Jay: As Black male educators, we offer numerous academic benefits for all students, especially Black students. We provide an effective and supportive learning environment that benefits all students, specifically Black students, as it relates to behavior, social, and academic development. We provide advocacy, support, and more representation for Black students. As a Black male educator, I have had the privilege to serve as a role model and father figure for many students. I have also been able to relate better to minority students and provide the necessary support, encouragement, and mentorship that they need to be successful.

Tyler: Within my classroom, I tend to interact with high-achieving students as I teach advanced courses. However, within these interactions with my students, I have seen an exceptional display of connectedness with the content. Through my discipline of science, there are many opportunities to embed what can be considered divisive context (i.e., sex and gender, the history and science of race, etc.). As a Black male educator who builds strong relationships with my students, I have facilitated thought-provoking and critical conversations related to these concepts. In speaking with my former students, they continue to come to me and say that I have been "the realest teacher" because of my willingness and openness to have these conversations. Allowing all my students the opportunity to express their opinions and ideas has provided growth which I believe would not come from many of my colleagues.

Scott: There lies a comfort in connecting with people who share profound similarities. That is true in most aspects of the human experience. Because of the shared historical condition Africans and their descendants have endured in America, Blacks who are not even acquainted with each other most often feel kinship and comfort in each other's presence. That is profoundly true for Black students. Having a Black educator to connect with provides a space for students to build a relationship with someone who understands their shared societal experiences and can provide guidance that can only come from one with historical and culturally familiar backgrounds. Black educators tend to better understand the cultural influences that manifest in Black students' behavioral and academic performance. Because of this innate understanding, there tends to be greater tolerance, patience, and willingness to connect with families. Research suggests that those factors, among others, are why Black students perform remarkably better with Black educators. In my experience as an educator and a colleague of Black educators, I have found these principles accurate and consistent throughout my career. This brief explanation does not suggest that white or other non-Black educators cannot positively impact Black students' educational experience. They do it every day, no different from a female teacher having an impact on a male student. However, research and personal experience support the notion that Black educators have a significant and positive impact on the education of Black students.

Joel: I have found this statement to be accurate because having a Black educator in the classroom allows for the students to have someone they can look up to and be a positive role model in their lives. I say that not only as a teacher but also as a former student. Throughout my K-12 education, I only had one Black teacher and she was an English teacher during my junior year of high school. Once I entered higher education institutions such as Morehouse College and North Carolina A&T State University, I found myself surrounded by many distinguished Black educators. As a result of that influence, I felt inspired to be better in my studies and perform well in my college career.

Michael: Having sat through hundreds of hours of professional development, a clip from Rita Pierson's TedTalk "Every Child Deserves a Champion" still stands out to me. One of my major takeaways from her talk was that students do not learn and grow from people that they do not like. When I think of the experiences of Black males in America, a society where we are often seen as threats, as hoodlums, as a population of folks only good at sports or entertainment, I believe that we understand the power of building and establishing relationships to prove doubters wrong. Black male educators empathize with the struggle, hardship, and challenges students face. With that, Black male educators understand that in order to help motivate and encourage students who have unfavorable upbringings, meaningful relationships must be built. Students need to feel trusted and, most importantly, students of color need to see that they can be more than their current circumstances. Black male educators are an anomaly. The fact that they have matriculated into a collegiate program, graduated, and are now making a living serves as inspiration for students who feel like they have no hope outside of their current reality. Black male educators know resilience, display curiosity, understand hardship, and share hope, making their presence in the classroom invaluable. Once students feel loved, heard, and inspired, they can begin to make academic strides that transcend even their most hopeful aspirations.

Steven: In many Black communities the police are white, the educators are white, and many authority figures are white, and this results in an issue of trust. Black families trust Black educators until they prove themselves not to be trustworthy. On the other hand, many Black families do not trust white educators until they prove that they are trustworthy. Another huge factor is relatability. Black educators can provide the inspiration, empathy, and tough love that impacts Black students for life.

*See below for dissertation citation.
Carter, G. M. (2020). *When they see us: A case study exploring culturally responsive school leadership in a midwestern suburban middle school* (Publication No. 27999343) [Doctoral dissertation, Indiana University]. ProQuest Dissertations & Theses Global.

41

Summary

The authors credit a sense of connectedness, relatability, and the ability to form close relationships as key reasons that they found success with their students and, particularly, their Black students. While students may find some comfort and familiarity in educators who look like them, there are certainly positive teacher-student relationships across racial lines. However, as Steven points out, there may be shared cultural norms that allow for trust to be established earlier between Black students and teachers. As such, when Black educators take a tough love approach students may believe that the actions come from a place of high expectations and belief in their abilities as opposed to questioning whether their teacher likes them.

Chapter 4 Reflection

Record your thoughts, notes, and takeaways below.

_____

_____

_____

_____

_____

_____

_____

_____

_____

_____

_____

_____

_____

_____

Chapter 5

David: We are currently living in a hostile political climate regarding social justice, police brutality, and systemic racism. This, all while our children are being reared in a society where Black males are not often seen in a positive light. Sadly, some people including young children are taught to fear Black men. Teachers of color serve as great role models not just for students of color but for all students. When Black male educators are an integral part of educational environments, this deconstructs stereotypes and creates more culturally relevant teaching environments. If children were exposed to Black male educators, especially in the early years of elementary school, it would help transform the negative narrative of how African American men are perceived in our local and global communities. Students and staff thrive when given opportunities to interact respectfully with people from other races and backgrounds. These relationships help disprove stereotypes and expose unconscious bias to create safe places for students and staff. When Black male educators are inspired and empowered, this will build support for changing attitudes, values, beliefs, and policies regarding the teaching of cultural sensitivity, educational equity, and embracing diversity. Ultimately, this will lead to increased academic achievement for all students.

Ernest: I have broken down a lot of stereotypes that my peers may have had about people of color, especially Black men. When I get to a new building it is always interesting to see how my peers interact with me as well as their level of comfort. That is just another layer of the pressure that comes along with being one of the few Black males in every building that I have ever worked in. Not only am I representing myself each day, but I am also representing Black men everywhere especially in education and in my district. I feel a kinship and shared purpose with my Black male counterparts, and we walk in that every day. I will always live and speak my truth, but it is not my job to make my colleagues comfortable in my presence; that will be up to them.

Fredrick: Since there are very few Black male educators, having a Black male working in the school can have a positive influence on all students' educational performance. Access to a Black male educator can provide an opportunity for students to learn to develop an understanding and appreciation for diversity. It can also show that educators are not a monolith. Black male educators bring a different perspective and approach to working with students.

Since many Black male educators have experienced prejudice and discrimination within the educational system, we can help disrupt these systems and malpractices to create a better and brighter future for students of all colors. Additionally, Black male educators often serve as trusted adults or mentors for students on top of fulfilling our job responsibilities. These mentorship opportunities allow students to feel a sense of belonging within the school community and can make a difference in students' motivation to achieve their goals.

Jay: Black male educators can enhance the school environment by supporting educational equity and addressing systemic racism in education. I have been able to cultivate relationships with students and staff of all ethnicities and backgrounds which has improved their knowledge and understanding about Black males and Black culture. I have also been able to challenge inaccurate stereotypes about Black male educators by addressing negative perceptions of Black men in general. This has allowed me to promote cultural awareness in my school environment by teaching students and staff about diverse perspectives. As a Black male educator, I serve as a role model and father figure for students of all ethnicities, not just for Black students.

Tyler: The presence of diversity promotes learning opportunities for all. Throughout my educational career, I have been a teacher for other teachers as well. That is, I have had to help my colleagues understand certain situations, give feedback on interactions, and provide ideas on the next steps. As I strive to do this within my career, my colleagues need to learn, grow, and develop their understanding as well. However, my ability to be that first example provides insights that allow them to take theory into practice. For my students, I get to be a leader, guide, mentor, and figure of success. My love for science came from my first Black male teacher. As such, I believe that having Black male teachers can help to inspire that desire to learn for all students, especially young Black students.

Scott: Any time people are exposed to those of different cultures, races, or backgrounds, there is an opportunity to build bridges of understanding and break down negative individual stereotypes and biases that may exist. White students need to have Black teachers and administrators because it exposes them to the perspectives of an adult educator who is Black and may have a different lens than what they may be exposed to at home or from most white teachers they likely had. It presents an opportunity to experience and foster lines of communication and appreciation that may not have been created otherwise. It is also beneficial for white students to be exposed to Black figures in positions of leadership and authority. More than ever, we live in an interconnected global society and share a world where people of color make up the overwhelming global racial majority. Here in the United States, the 2020 U.S. Census reported that for children under 18, the collective people of color are the majority, and the collective people of color in the totality of all ages will become the majority in America as early as 2040. Therefore, not only does having a Black teacher or administrator create relationship-building opportunities for white students, but experiencing a Black person in a position of authority also prepares white students to enter society and an economy where people of color are increasing in population and representation in industry leadership.

Joel: One way that Black male educators enhance the environment for all students is by offering a different perspective on how to teach students. For example, not only do I teach mathematics at my school, but I also advise my school's chess club. I use the game of chess to help my students learn not only how to use strategy but also how to apply critical thinking skills that are applicable in the classroom and when they reach adulthood.

Michael: Frequently, I find myself in spaces where staff are more reserved when it comes to speaking their mind. This is the opposite of what I am known for. I like to believe that speaking up is a part of who I am. At a district meeting, I remember speaking up and advocating for higher-level administrators to be cognizant of the experiences of minority leaders in the predominantly white district. I referenced the experiences of people of color, men in an elementary setting, and women in a high school setting. Following the meeting, a colleague of color sent me an email expressing his thanks for my willingness to speak up. He shared that he has sat in many meetings wanting to share his thoughts but had not mustered up the courage to do so. I firmly believe that Black male educators have a presence that promotes an environment of resilience, hope, advocacy, and courage. There is a boldness that fills the atmosphere when Black male educators are present.

Steven: Early in my career, I thought I could only impact children who looked like me. I was misguided. Black male educators make a positive impact on Black students as well as all students. I serve as an administrator in an elementary school with about 600 students and at least 15 different cultures. We live in a world where stereotypes are driven by social media and news from a phone or tablet. For many children, these outlets are the only window into Black culture. Our presence not only enhances the educational environment, but it counters stereotypical definitions of Blackness. I aim to challenge assumptions about what it means to be a Black male in this society.

Summary

Black male educators benefit Black students while also forming deep relationships with students across races. Many of the authors speak of stereotypes that they challenge and defy because of their presence as a Black male educator. This can be especially true with non-Black students whose real-life experiences with Black men may be limited causing them to have preconceived notions of Black males based on stereotypes. Some authors also shared how they have helped their colleagues to better understand and navigate situations by providing necessary cultural context that, left unaddressed, would keep barriers in place. While Black male educators often find themselves having to provide this cultural insight to their colleagues, as Tyler notes, non-Black educators must also be willing to take it upon themselves to do the work of becoming more culturally responsive and competent.

> *"Early in my career, I thought I could only impact children who looked like me. I was misguided. Black male educators make a positive impact on Black students as well as all students."*
> -Steven

Chapter 5 Reflection

Record your thoughts, notes, and takeaways below.

_____

_____

_____

_____

_____

_____

_____

_____

_____

_____

_____

_____

_____

_____

Chapter 6
Question: Why are there so few Black males in education? How do you think we can increase our representation?

David: Since there is a lack of Black male role models in education, many young boys never perceive themselves working in a school setting nor discern their potential to influence the next generation of young leaders. I did not have a Black male teacher until my junior year in high school. I believe this lack of representation has led to education not being a top career choice for men of color and, unfortunately, those who do choose education often leave after a few years in the classroom. Too often, African American men with aspirations for moving out of the classroom into leadership positions are passed over for promotions. This is especially true if classroom management and cultivating student relationships is a strength for them. We are made to feel guilty by leaving the classroom, as if we are letting students down. To increase our representation in the field of education, policymakers, universities, districts, schools, educators, and the greater educational community must be committed to making it a reality with financial revenue specifically designated for the cause. The solution lies in strategic processes concerning recruiting, training, hiring, mentoring, and retaining highly qualified Black male educators. We must engage current Black male educators in ongoing dialogue regarding barriers and other challenges they face. There is no better way than to hear from the voices of those in the trenches to put structures in place so that Black male educators are fully prepared, valued, listened to, and supported so that they may flourish in classrooms across America.

Ernest: There are several reasons that there are so few Black males in education. One factor is the amount of training and education that you must obtain for average to low pay. It took me over 20 years in my profession to get to a six-figure salary. Many of my friends from college were at that salary within five years of starting their careers. Also, we must improve the working conditions for all teachers, especially those working in large urban districts where many new teachers end up. Education is one of the few professions that does not set up its new employees for success. Oftentimes, young Black teachers will be put into situations with the most challenging students and the least number of resources. I am not sure how to increase the representation unless the school districts in this country get serious about the working conditions for teachers.

Fredrick: Traditional gender roles within our society have influenced the career choices of men and women. For example, men are often encouraged to enter STEM-related fields. Historically, most primary and secondary educators have been women. Serving as a teacher was one of the few positions that women were allowed to do, and teaching was largely considered to be more of a nurturing role. Black culture had adhered to these traditional gender roles as well, and Black men were not encouraged to enter the field. The lack of Black male representation in education perpetuates the cycle of many Black men not wanting to enter a field that historically has never looked like them.

A key component to helping increase Black male representation in education is through recruitment and helping young Black men see the value of their presence within educational environments. If Black students see how they can make a difference as an educator that might encourage them to become one themselves. By Black male educators having a positive impact on Black male students, this may inspire the next generation of Black males to consider a position in education. Additionally, speaking to high school and college students about the positive influence they can have on students can impact their decision to enter the field of education.

Jay: Education has historically been a female-dominated field, made up primarily of white women. Traditionally, Black men have aimed to provide for themselves and their families in other fields with higher wages. There are ways that we can increase our representation including recruitment and retention, mentorship, advocating for equity in policy, and promoting teacher diversity. There must be better ways and strategies to improve the interest of Black males and increase their involvement in the educational field. This will then allow Black males to see themselves represented well in education and to see the importance of their role in the lives of all students. Mentorship is very important for Black males so that they can receive effective training to support and guide more Black males in hopes of encouraging them to join this profession.

Tyler: The minimal representation of Black males in education is due, in part, to our capitalist society. As a teacher and a student, it is known that you will not be making hundreds of thousands of dollars each year. We teach our students that to be successful in this world, you must make money. Therefore, why would being a teacher seem to be a possible outcome of their education? We as teachers need to focus on promoting the benefits of teaching. Too many times students only see the struggles of education: being run down, not having enough resources, etc. As Black male educators, we need to highlight how teaching is an uplifting and powerful profession. We also need to teach and provide opportunities for students to cultivate a spirit of community and service. Capitalism prompts me to compare myself to another to determine my success. However, as a teacher, I determine my success in the number of students I reach each year. I define my success by those who come back years later to say, "You made a difference."

Scott: The first aspect to consider is that Black male college students are proportionally underrepresented no matter the field of study. In education specifically, the number of candidates of all races enrolled in the colleges of education around the country is falling to near-crisis levels. According to the National Center for Educational Statistics, as recently as the 2017-2018 school year, Black educators accounted for less than seven percent of the teaching field nationally. Children aspire to become what they see or are exposed to in television or social media outlets. It is not uncommon for Black students, especially those in a suburban or rural school district, to travel through their K-12 educational journey and never be exposed to a Black teacher. If they are, the chances are greater that the Black educator is a female. My education occurred in an urban school district where higher concentrations of Black educators are generally found. In my K-12 experience, I had one Black male teacher. To be fair, I had several Black female teachers in elementary, middle, and high school, but only one male. Therefore, few Black boys aspire to be something they never see or experience. The unintended message they receive may be that the teaching profession is not attractive or desirable for Black males. Another barrier for Black boys is the belief that educators do not make much money. In my experience teaching urban Black boys, many dreamed of playing professional sports, namely football or basketball. For most of them, their athletic heroes amounted to the only celebrity millionaires they could relate to. For them, being a teacher seemed like something less than a "cool" career.

Fixing this trend goes beyond individual school districts developing "Grow Your Own" type programs or scrounging for a partnership with a local college. It would take a systemic shift in legislation and policy that incentivizes college-going Black male students to choose the education field. It would take concentrated mentorships, impactful scholarships, student loan forgiveness programs, special tax credits, job placement programs, housing allowances or deductions, etc.

Short of such a widespread, systematic effort, school districts throughout America will keep spinning on the same treadmill, hoping their homegrown programs will create a few more Black male educator candidates for districts to compete for.

Joel: The reason why there are very few Black males in education is due to a lack of opportunity. In my current building, I am one of two Black male teachers for elementary and middle school. Considering schools like to highlight their diversity in terms of the student body, the best way to increase staff representation would be to provide more opportunities to allow Black males to teach in the classroom. This can also help students to have Black male role models which could impact their future aspirations.

Michael: In 2019, I joined the Digital Promise Teacher of Color Advisory Council. My role as a council member was to work with other teachers across Western Pennsylvania to identify ways that school leaders could recruit and retain teachers of color. Some of the common themes that came up during our multiple conversations were the lack of support teachers of color felt from administrators, the lack of leadership opportunities for teachers of color, the daily microaggressions teachers of color faced, and the fact that there was no incentive to stay in education. We also discussed how teaching is not presented to students of color in a manner that is inviting or exciting to them like you see in the entertainment business. One solution to increase the representation of teachers of color in the field of education is by creating financial incentives for high school seniors or college students to pursue an education degree. Another solution was to establish support groups for teachers of color within school districts to create a sense of community. This would help retain Black male educators, allowing for more to be in the field. Ultimately, there is no real science to recruiting and retaining Black male educators. However, if this is a problem that we are going to solve, we need to continue working with current and former Black male educators and use their testimonies to find ways to recruit more Black men in the field.

Steven: According to the 2021 National Teacher and Principal Survey, less than two percent of public school teachers in the United States were Black men. Why are there so few Black men in education? There are three major factors. First, we are not invited into the field of education like white women are. From an early age, many Black boys are told they would make a great athlete but are rarely told they would make a great teacher, doctor, or any other profession. From my experience, Black male educators are either inspired by another Black teacher early in life, or they are trying to spare other Black children the traumatic educational experience that they had. Second, education is a female-dominated field. Like nursing, I believe men in general avoid careers that are monopolized by women and viewed as a feminine role. Society generally identifies childcare or caregiver roles as feminine and I believe this discourages men, especially Black men. Third, education is an undervalued career. Many Black men do not see education as a field that can financially sustain them and their families. When I left the urban district for the suburban district, there was close to a $15,000 salary increase. We can clearly see what society values by looking at the money and time invested.

To increase our representation, we must intentionally tell Black boys that they should be educators or that they would make great educators. As a society, we have to change the dominant narratives about education. We need to celebrate and honor men in education. We must speak positively to our Black boys and encourage them to believe in themselves even when society doubts them and systemic factors in education keep them out.

Summary

The lack of Black male educators means that many Black male students are not taught by someone who looks like them. As such, these students may not envision themselves as future educators so, instead, they aspire to become more like the Black male figures heavily featured in media and pop culture (musicians, athletes, actors, etc.). Some authors note that low teacher pay contributes to Black men seeking other career paths. To increase the number of Black male educators, the authors call for better recruitment and mentorship programs. Also, as Scott notes, there should be additional scholarships and financial incentives to remove systemic barriers and increase the appeal of pursuing the profession.

Chapter 6 Reflection

Record your thoughts, notes, and takeaways below.

_____

_____

_____

_____

_____

_____

_____

_____

_____

_____

_____

_____

_____

_____

Chapter 7
Question: How do you navigate being in a space where few, if any, educators share your identity?

David: Being an African American educator can be a lonely place and even more so for a Black male. Early in my career, I was fortunate enough to have been mentored by experienced, passionate, and devoted educators who believed in me and were totally committed to my success. Twenty-plus years later, I am grateful I chose to hear and heed their wisdom. Their unwavering dedication, honest feedback, and true authenticity made a tremendous impact on my personal and professional life. Their ultimate goal was to ensure the next generation of young educators was fully prepared to accept the baton and carry on the work of educating the future leaders of the world. Because of this type of mentorship, I have acquired skills to successfully navigate in spaces where few, if any, educators share my identity. It taught me the importance and necessity of finding my tribe which established my foundation and provided me with a sense of responsibility and accountability. It is important to maintain a core group of mentors and educators with whom you can share ideas, discuss issues, brainstorm solutions, and vent when needed. There is nothing better than having intimate, face-to-face, wisdom-sharing sessions with people who share the same spirit, purpose, vision, and mindset. I need people who will have my back and tell me the good, bad, and ugly regarding my performance while pushing me forward to my destiny. All of this has proven critical for my success.

Ernest: One of the things that you have to learn to deal with as a Black male educator is the fact that you will not have many safe spaces at your workplace. You will have to create your own network of people who understand your daily struggles and challenges. This is not to say that you cannot form very strong personal and professional relationships with some of your non-Black colleagues. However, if you are looking for someone who understands some of the specific challenges of what it is like to be a Black male educator, they are few and far between. You will have to create your own support network that you can reach out to when you feel like no one in your building truly understands your plight.

Fredrick: When there are only a few Black men in any space, we tend to gravitate toward each other as a way of acknowledgment. It has been helpful for me to connect with fellow Black educators during my career to build community and a sense of belonging. As I make connections with my Black colleagues, I feel a sense of inclusion as we often share similar experiences and perspectives. Not only do I seek out these opportunities for myself, but I also try to be a connection for my Black colleagues, so they too feel supported. I understand the feeling of being the only person of color in the room and try to make sure others do not feel isolated due to their racial identity. While I still find myself in educational spaces where I am the only Black male, I no longer attempt to de-emphasize my racial identity in these spaces. I now permit myself to be myself by not assimilating and conforming to traditional Eurocentric standards.

Jay: As a Black male educator and administrator, I realize that I am navigating in spaces where there are few educators and administrators who share the same identity or ethnicity as me. I understand that there are benefits and challenges to this position. Of the benefits, I realize that one of them is that I am in a unique position to educate others about the perception of Black male educators and how capable we are as leaders when given an opportunity. I also understand the challenges in this position include discrimination and prejudice, and the lack of support from others who do not understand my identity. Staying true to my faith and beliefs as well as creating balance has been key to my success in spaces where others do not share my identity. I have built a strong core team of current and former Black male educators who provide support, training, and guidance regarding this unique position. I am confident in who I am and my ability as a leader and educator. I believe that God has placed me in these spaces for a purpose, and I will allow Him to use me to reach, educate, and love the people in the spaces that I am called to serve.

Tyler: Being the lone Black male has been a struggle for me throughout my life. As I grew up in a predominantly white neighborhood, I rarely had people around me who shared my identity. Therefore, as a teacher, it feels normal because I focus not on myself but on my students. I am living my life and doing what is necessary for me to be happy, but I had to learn many of those things on my own in school. To cope with my struggle, I focus on being an asset to the Black students I teach and provide them with as many resources as I can to promote a healthy connection to their identity.

Scott: When I became an administrator in a local suburban school district, I faced an adjustment period working almost exclusively with white colleagues. In the urban district where I taught, my school had several Black teachers and nearly an all-Black student body. In that environment, surrounded by people of similar cultural and racial attributes, I experienced mental comfort and weightlessness to the extent that I did not notice the absence or scarcity of white colleagues. In the suburban district I joined, there were two Black teachers on staff, both of whom I knew previously, and our Black male principal. The principal was once my high school principal. The remaining hundred or so staff members were white. While they were all welcoming and kind to me, I always felt that I needed to keep my guard up and present an image I believed they expected. I brought with me the desire for their staff to accept me, and I wanted to fit in with the school and community's culture. I went so far as to swap my dress pants and Stacy Adams shoes for khakis and Buster Browns. I cringe and laugh to think about that today. I carried with me the anxiety of whether they would judge me by a fair standard, and that burden was always present, whether I realized it or not.

Over time, I built meaningful relationships with white colleagues and have become very comfortable with who I am as a person and with my value systems. Being one of but a few Black males in a sea of white colleagues is something I have grown accustomed to. However, I always notice. I notice how few people there are surrounding me who identify like me. I notice the same comfort that white colleagues enjoy that I had when surrounded by Black teachers and students. It does not bother me to be among the few, but I notice. I have gotten close enough with a few of my white colleagues to trade blunt ideologies about race and culture. Further, I have gotten them to notice which is something they admittedly never did before.

Joel: When it comes to navigating a space where there are no Black male educators, I rely on what I learned when I was a student. Before going to Morehouse College where people who share my identity would surround me, it was normal for me to be one of a few Black students in class from K-12th grade. Even though I am often among a small fraction of people who share my identity, I do my best to form a bond with those like me. For example, I was intentional about forming a bond with the music teacher at my school who is also a Black male. When I was a paraprofessional at my school, the music teacher asked me to help run the school's drum club. This collaboration ultimately benefited students. What we lack in quantity as Black male educators, we more than make up for in the quality of our instruction and how we inspire our students.

Michael: Since I began my time as an educator, the phrase "sense of belonging" has been something that has floated around in every district I have worked in. I have always challenged that phrase, but my wondering remains the same: Who is this sense of belonging for? Being the only Black male educator in all white spaces or even being the only Black male educator in urban spaces is exhausting. Navigating these spaces is challenging, especially when no one can relate to some of the experiences that I face daily. When I was teaching, I remember being told by a student that I made everything about race. This left me questioning what I did, and I wondered who I could share this with who might understand how hurtful this was. I decided to speak with the school counselor hoping that he would address the student. However, I was disappointed that I did not feel like I could take this to my administrator as I was not sure that they would see the problem. To help me navigate these spaces, I collaborate with colleagues in other districts who look like me and work with allies who can empathize with my experiences. Most of all, I remind myself that regardless of who looks like me, our students' lives can only be changed when we work together.

Steven: My passion for education and serving others has influenced the way I navigate a space where few, if any, educators share my identity. To make an impact in education, your heart must be in it. If that passion for education is burning in your heart and you have a true love for serving others, you can make your way through being the only one.

You must maintain a growth mindset and remain focused on being an instructional leader.

Summary
To combat the challenges and loneliness that come with being a Black male educator, many authors expressed the importance of bonding and networking with other Black male educators. In some cases, this requires establishing networks across buildings and districts. These networks, whether formal or informal, enable Black males to collaborate, receive guidance, vent, and be challenged in a safe manner. This allows for both personal and professional growth. Some authors note the importance of building strong relationships with peers across racial lines. Scott forms close relationships with trusted allies of other races to exchange critical dialogue. Jay cultivates relationships with non-Black colleagues to help open and shape minds.

Chapter 7 Reflection
Record your thoughts, notes, and takeaways below.

_____

_____

_____

_____

_____

_____

_____

_____

_____

_____

_____

_____

_____

Chapter 8

Question: How do you use your voice to combat deficit thinking and biases that some of your colleagues may have about students of color?

David: As a classically trained singer, I know that the human voice is a beautiful and powerful tool whether it is used as a musical instrument or used to create awareness, understanding, sensitivity, connection, healing, wholeness, or unity. While speaking up is risky both personally and professionally, I am fully cognizant of my obligation to wisely and appropriately lift my voice to help combat the deficit thinking and biases some of my colleagues have regarding underrepresented students. I advocate for those students by educating coworkers about implicit bias, cultural competency, and achievement gaps. Through personal and group conversations, I help educators fully understand the dire need to consistently and equitably expose Black students to the richness of knowledge while holding them to high expectations and the importance of looking beyond the color of their skin. My goal is to aid, empower, and support educators in building trust with students while they nurture and inspire students toward their destinies. Once educators have cultivated relationships with students of color, students are more likely to trust them and meet their expectations.

Ernest: No matter what role I have had in my 25-year career in education, I have never been afraid to voice my opinion or speak up when I have seen or heard something that I did not agree with. This has especially applied to my experiences with students and families of color. Oftentimes, they are viewed in a certain way by the dominant majority in education. I have sometimes been the only voice in the room that represented the Black population and families in my school and educational spaces. As a leader, I must create training opportunities and professional development sessions to specifically address deficit thinking and the damage that can have on our students of color. I remind my staff all the time that I do not need anyone trying to "save" my students; I just need my students to be educated. There is a huge difference between empathy and sympathy. We need to lead with empathy and understand that the path of all students may be different. However, we should never lower the bar or expectations for our students. Sympathy takes you down the path of lowered expectations and dangerous educational stereotypes.

Fredrick: Everyone holds biases whether we are aware of them or not. Some of these biases tend to influence how we interact with our students and can create a self-fulfilling prophecy, especially for those of vulnerable diverse groups. Whether it was students of color or English Language Learners, I have witnessed how my colleagues' assumptions impacted these students' educational experiences. It has been important for me as a Black male educator to speak up in these instances and discuss how our biases may influence how we approach students' education and the decisions we make. I attempt to engage my colleagues in conversations that bring awareness to how we may combat our personal biases and become more cognizant of the factors impacting our decisions. Additionally, sharing my personal experiences as a Black male growing up in a historically discriminatory educational system has helped put this topic in perspective for many of my colleagues. I have found that allowing the space to share and discuss real-world examples tends to resonate with people more effectively than a generic training that may be less applicable.

Jay: To combat deficit thinking and biases towards students of color, we must challenge our colleagues and encourage them to evaluate their own biases. I use my voice and position to increase professional development opportunities around deficit thinking, biases, and stereotypes. In this way, my colleagues are exposed to these concepts and how influential they are when serving our students. The goal is to enable educators to evaluate their feelings and assumptions regarding the academic and behavioral performances of students of color. This will help inaccurate stereotypes to be corrected and create a more equitable environment for all students. Professional development is an essential part of teaching non-Black educators about the culture and mannerisms associated with students of color. More importantly, the professional development sessions can emphasize the importance of cultural competency and bias reduction.

Tyler: Utilizing my voice as one of the few Black male educators in my building can be difficult, but I have found that repetition is key. However, I should clarify, that there is a large contingent of my colleagues who see the achievement gap as more of an opportunity gap. The times in which I have had to utilize my voice come in larger group discussions. By using my authority as a Black man who recently completed a master's degree in diversity and equity, many people listen. I am not sure if I can attribute that to being a male in a predominately female career, or if it is due to my demonstration of knowledge. While there is always a handful of those who still cannot internalize these concepts, the majority have accepted these ideals and are moving towards a more equitable approach to educating our students of color.

Scott: Humor is my voice. I use it to make a point that may be uncomfortable otherwise. I use it to teach, and I use it to highlight hypocrisy and inequality. Not every situation lends itself to a humorous response, but it is a tool I have found effective. At other times, I rely on previously built relationships to advise or redirect. Sometimes, a sharper response is warranted. Using my voice is a responsibility to advocate for our children of color, many of whom do not have anyone to advocate for them. In my position, I can examine and present critical data points to foster discussion and action. I can authorize professional development, recommend building and district goals and, in extreme cases, proceed with any necessary disciplinary measures.

I am currently the assistant superintendent in a rapidly diversifying school district. In 2023, students of color comprised 50% of our K-12 population and are the collective majority in nearly half of our school buildings. Current trends predict that white students will be the collective minority population in our district within two to three years. Yet, our teaching staff is over 90% white and, in several of our buildings, represents 100% of the staff. Our schools and community embrace our diverse student population, and our Building Equity Teams have worked diligently to train our staff to address our students' academic and social-emotional needs. As we review and decide on initiatives, programs, and resources, I must use my voice to help ensure that all aspects of our students are considered and represented.

Joel: When it comes to combating deficit thinking and biases towards students of color, I try to instill confidence and determination within my students to improve their achievement so that the results speak for themselves. Considering I teach math which can be difficult for many students, it is very easy for them to think they are dumb because they struggle with it. Daily, I remind my students that they are smart and capable of learning the course material. This mentality does not sink in right away but, with patience and hard work, students eventually see the fruits of their labor as the school year progresses. One student that comes to mind struggled during the first semester but received an A by the end of the school year. Such instances demonstrate what students can achieve when teachers choose to invest in them instead of engaging in deficit thinking.

Michael: One thing I have heard throughout my career is that some students of color do not want to learn. This way of thinking is belittling, but it speaks less about the student and more about the narrow-minded educator who lacks confidence in their teaching. The reality is that students of color are great learners, but they need teachers who believe in them. Further, they require educators who do not hold them responsible for factors beyond their control. For example, take a high school student who is repeatedly late to school from working an overnight shift to support her family. It is unfair to state that this student does not care about her education; instead, she is prioritizing the needs of her loved ones. In another example, take a young boy who acts out in class but performs well on assessments. It is unethical to exclude him from gifted classes due to behavior challenges. Instead, we must find ways to offer enrichment opportunities that can lead to less negative behaviors. The best way to combat deficit thinking and to counter biases is by seeing and responding to the needs of the whole child, and reminding all teachers that all students can learn. The real question that educators with deficit thinking should ask is about the effectiveness of their own teaching practices.

Steven: My voice is not as loud as my actions, so I combat deficit thinking by being intentional about the ways that I discuss the students I serve with my colleagues. If they hear me speaking negatively about "problem" students, it will reinforce the deficit narratives they already possess about these students and families. I need to push my colleagues past their own biases and challenge them to see their students' potential and not their problems.

Summary

Several authors expressed that using their voice to combat deficit thinking and biases is a responsibility of Black male educators. This is because they can bring awareness to their colleagues' biases that perhaps they are unable to see themselves. Further, Black male educators are positioned to serve as advocates for their students and can leverage their own experiences within the education system to be a voice for students and families. As leaders within their schools and districts, authors Tyler and Michael use their voices to shape staff discussions and school initiatives by promoting culturally responsive practices. Ultimately, this helps educators to reflect upon their pedagogy and implement more equitable policies and approaches resulting in improved experiences for all students.

Chapter 8 Reflection

Record your thoughts, notes, and takeaways below.

_____

_____

_____

_____

_____

_____

_____

_____

_____

_____

_____

_____

_____

Chapter 9

Question: Share a story about a student or family that has had a profound impact on you.

David: On any given day, a second-grade boy being raised by his great-grandparents would become physically aggressive with other students and with teachers. It was common for him to yell, run around the room, and throw objects across the room, disrupting learning and making it an unsafe environment. Often, the classroom had to be evacuated for safety concerns. His great-grandmother, who was in her late seventies, would weep uncontrollably while relaying that she had seen these same behaviors at home as well as church. The boy's behavior even got him kicked out of the children's ministry program and the family had to find another place of worship. She was gravely concerned about her great-grandson's future especially because of her advancing age, her husband's failing health, the rejection of a mother addicted to drugs, and a grandmother who had no interest in being involved in his life. In each of our conversations, she would apologize to me expressing that she did not know why he was acting this way.

At that point, I realized the boy needed to know he was special and part of something bigger than himself. In my plan to set him up for success, we would touch base each morning, and I would stop in the classroom and sit next to him during instruction. If he needed to talk or take a break, he could ask his teacher to come to my office. That year, his great-grandparents, teachers, and I saw great growth in the student as he slowly began to calm himself, partake in the learning process, and become more accountable for his actions.

Ernest: As a middle school administrator, I had a set of brothers who often would end up in my office for various incidents of disrespectful behavior which is often a buzzword used by some teachers to remove students from class. I would work with the boys over and over on how to express themselves, but to do so in a way that would not get them sent to the office. I spent hours and hours with those boys and, eventually, they figured it out and became successful in middle school. Their mom wrote me the nicest card at the end of that school year and brought me several neckties as a way to express her gratitude to me for taking care of her boys. The boys went on to high school and began to fall into the same cycle that they did when they were in middle school. Their mother would still reach out to me to try and support her boys. The story did not have a happy ending, and I am often left wondering how their paths might have been different if they had a high school staff member who connected with them the same way that I did. Their high school did not have any Black male teachers and there was only one Black male staff member in the entire school. Was that the main reason that they regressed? I often struggle with that answer.

Fredrick: The COVID-19 pandemic had a significant impact on many of our students' developmental functioning, especially our preschool and kindergarten students who were attending school for the first time. During my fourth year as a school psychologist, a kindergarten student appeared to have lacked a significant number of skills that prevented him from successfully transitioning into a structured learning environment. Once more was learned about the student and his background, many of these concerns made sense in context. This student's father had passed away a few years before and his mother reported that she was not emotionally available to support him and his development as she struggled with substance abuse. This student's story made me realize that, as educators, we had an opportunity to potentially change the trajectory of this student's life and provide him with the support that he required to be successful. With evidenced-based interventions, consistency, and countless hours of support, our school team was able to help him get on grade level by the end of the school year. He learned skills to help him regulate his emotions and, overall, he became a better student. His mother reported that she noticed a significant difference in his educational progress and functioning while at home and expressed her gratitude. Moments like these are what keep me energized and motivated to continue to support my students. Regardless of their trauma or background, all students are worth fighting for.

Jay: Among the many students that have impacted and influenced my development as a leader and educator, a Black female student stands out in particular. This girl performed well academically but struggled socially and behaviorally, especially with white adults. There were a few occasions where she felt misunderstood with one specific white female teacher, and it resulted in multiple confrontations. One day during a transition between classes, I noticed her crying in the hallway and walked her to a less crowded area of the hallway. After learning about what transpired between her and the aforementioned teacher, I calmed her down and reminded her of the academic and behavioral expectations for students and teachers. We both then met with the teacher and discussed the situation along with the perspectives of both the teacher and student. Although the student still encountered some issues in school –largely due to some dynamics in her home environment– her response to adults improved and she also improved academically.

Tyler: I had a student in my second year, who is currently one of my lab assistants, and he continues to inspire me in my profession. He is a young Black male who was going through a regular biology class for the second time. At the beginning of the year, he admitted that he did not enjoy science because he felt that he could not be successful at it. Throughout that year he grew as a learner and watching him become more confident has been inspiring. He is a student who may not excel in many of the things that he does. Yet, he continues to work hard to be better. At the end of last year, he said I was the first teacher to inspire him to want to learn. Throughout this year I have had in-depth conversations with him about what it means to be a Black man in America, and how we must navigate systems that have historically tried to hold us back. He is a student who has deep insights into what it means to be a good person, and his growth has reminded me that the simplest things in a classroom can mean the world to students.

Scott: During my tenure as a teacher, I had the honor of teaching a young man who tended to be the favorite student of all his teachers. I cannot recall anyone, staff or student, who did not genuinely like this young man. He was an accomplished multi-sport athlete and a solid student. Still, his most impressive features were the personality and character traits he carried that teachers wished upon their own children. Forever wearing a toothy smile, he held firm to traditional values of respect, faithfully answering adults with "Yes, Sir," or "Yes, Ma'am." He married his high school sweetheart, who may have been the only student who surpassed his impeccable character. She was remarkable. I had the honor of being her teacher as well. She was the sort of person who could lift your spirits merely by the way she said, "Good morning." Tragedy struck the young couple when she passed away unexpectedly late in her first pregnancy due to medical complications. In a terribly tragic moment, this young man lost his wife and his unborn child. Everyone who knew them felt heartbroken. If life ever seemed cruel and unfair, it was then. The manner in which he carried on with grace was nothing short of miraculous. His friends and family circled him and held him up at a time when he could not stand alone. He went on to dedicate his life to social services and has risen to be a respected community leader. He now heads a significant social service agency in a large and thriving southern American city. He found love again, and he and his wife have a wonderful family with two beautiful children. My former student is an inspiration to me, not so much for his achievements in life but because of how he survived and thrived in his journey.

Joel: One family that has had a profound impact on me was a mother and daughter from my time as a long-term substitute teacher. During the spring semester that year, I was teaching Honors Geometry to this student. After a few weeks had passed, I received an email from the mother of the student. She was actually on staff at the school and said that her daughter spoke very highly of me. Not only was she able to understand everything I was teaching, but she was able to successfully answer her questions. This was a moment I cherished when starting my career as an educator because it was reassurance that I was able to make a difference in a student's life by showing that math does not have to be overwhelming.

Michael: During my time as an administrator in the inner city, I met a fourth grader who was raised with his mom until drugs took over her life. He eventually went to stay with a family friend who would serve as his foster parent while his mother worked to get clean. The student always referred to me as Dad, telling me that he never had a real father and he looked forward to spending time with me. The problem was he would do things to get in trouble so he could come to my office. One day, I witnessed him having a major episode where he was throwing things and putting himself and others in danger. He went on to explain that he was hoping to be placed back with his mom; instead, the incident landed him in juvenile court, and he felt like his life was ruined. His biological mother visited the school, and I watched as he wept in her arms, wanting to be back with his mom. This moment had a major impact on me for multiple reasons. For the first time, I felt like my past experiences truly allowed me to empathize with this young boy. This moment showed me the significance of why my being an educator, even with all my baggage, can be an asset since I can relate to and inspire little Black boys who look like me. I was also reminded that many students enter our buildings with significant baggage. It is our duty to ensure that students' needs are being met socially and emotionally, and this must occur before we can impact them academically.

Steven: I have had the privilege of building relationships with students that have lasted beyond the school year. I have gathered so many stories I do not know which one to choose. During my first year as a teacher, I had a student who could not tell the difference between a letter and a number. However, by year's end, he was reading above grade level. His family asked me to be his godfather when he was in first grade. He has since graduated high school but is still part of my family and looks to me as a mentor. While I was a high school wrestling coach, I met a skinny ninth grader who, after the day we met, would not let me out of his sight. After doing grade checks one week, I noticed his grade point average had slipped below 1.9. I was pretty tough on him, but I was the kind of coach who did not just focus on winning. I focused on building young men through our team's core values which promoted truth, perseverance, and support. After feeling my disappointment, this young man went from a 1.9 to a 3.6 in the following semester. During his junior year, he earned the award for the highest grade point average and was named the most valuable player on the wrestling team. The reason he made an impact on me is that despite several adverse childhood experiences, he never gave up. He gave me a reason to keep coaching. In fact, right before he went to college, he asked me to legally adopt him. Today, he is a computer science major at Central State University still fighting to make a difference in his life and the people around him.

Summary

The impactful stories that left a lasting impression on the authors were made possible because of the deep investment that these Black men made in their students. The authors looked beyond the behaviors and grades to better understand the human beings and the circumstances behind them. The most impactful students were often navigating traumas and situations that no child should have to face. The authors extended support and mentorship to these students and often their families to help them succeed. In many instances, this support not only changed the students but also the educators by validating the important work that they do.

Chapter 9 Reflection
Record your thoughts, notes, and takeaways below.

_____

_____

_____

_____

_____

_____

_____

_____

_____

_____

_____

_____

_____

_____

Chapter 10
Question: What keeps you returning year after year?

David: Teachers are leaving the education field at alarming rates. Due to today's challenges in the educational system and the effects of the COVID-19 pandemic, many educators are no longer finding education to be a fulfilling career. Yet, I regard education as my true vocation while still finding joy in helping to change the trajectory of young leaders from communities that are similar to mine. There is an incipient generation filled with a myriad of possibilities that are counting on me to make a difference by fulfilling my God-given purpose. What better arena than a school setting?

While embracing my calling may be scary and come with many challenges and barriers, it is worth the risks. Contemplating the scholastic issues of today and after having children and grandchildren of my own, I resolve that children are 100% of our future. As such, I have a longing zeal to inspire future generations of young people. Children are most deserving of the investment of our concentrated time, resources, and energy. I wholeheartedly relish the quote attributed to African American abolitionist Frederick Douglass who declared, "It is easier to build strong children than to repair broken men."

Ernest: This work is extremely personal for me, and this job is too important for me to leave it up to anyone else. Education has literally changed the entire trajectory of my life. It has provided me with the opportunity to travel the world and have a life that I would have never dreamed of growing up in Youngstown, Ohio. My goal each day is to do all that I can to give my students the opportunity to be whatever they want to be in life. Education is something that no one can ever take away from them. That is why I must keep showing up year after year.

Fredrick: Many of my students come from underprivileged backgrounds where resources and support may be limited in comparison to their counterparts. Educators often serve as one of the few trusted adults in these students' lives and I understand the importance of stability and consistency of those who support them. Despite many of the challenges I have faced while working in education, I return to my role each year to support my students' academic and personal goals. I ultimately want to make a difference and help contribute to my students' overall well-being. As a school psychologist, one of my goals is to communicate to students that despite the hardships they may be experiencing, there is someone at school who they can always rely on for support. Many educators are aware that to combat adverse childhood experiences, protective factors are needed to help a child overcome those experiences. I strive to be one of those protective factors for my students by helping them learn to persevere through obstacles that may come their way.

Jay: There are various reasons why I return to this profession year after year. One reason includes my dedication to helping others and my desire to make a positive impact on the lives of young people. I strongly believe that God has gifted me with a passion for our youth, and I will continue to allow Him to use me to reach them. I believe that I have been created to make a difference in the lives of our students, schools, and communities. The feedback from students, staff, and families that I have had the privilege of serving affirms that I am having a positive impact. I have also had the opportunity to meet some great leaders, learners, and educators which has turned into a community of support and collaboration. These types of experiences and relationships will continue to build and improve the education system while making it more attractive and attainable for future Black male educators.

Tyler: One factor that keeps me returning each year is knowing that my students are relying on me. I have several students who sign up for my classes to have me as their teacher. Some I have already built connections with, and others I have never met. Yet, the sentiment remains the same from those who take my classes because of me. They say that I am a fair teacher who strives to build positive relationships with students. These types of comments drive me to continue. Finally, I keep returning because change has not fully permeated yet. I see shifts in thinking and interacting that I hope will continue, but I cannot and will not give up on my efforts to get students to believe in themselves and know that they can succeed and make a positive difference in the world.

Scott: My answer to this question has changed throughout my career. As a young teacher in my twenties, I returned because it was the profession of my college degree, and it paid the bills. Also, as a basketball coach, the excitement of the possibilities of the next season kept me motivated. I loved interacting with my students and thrived off their energy. Yet, my career satisfaction was not enough to keep me from entertaining other careers. After my fourth year of teaching, my position was eliminated due to a reduction in force resulting from dwindling student enrollment. I could have stayed knowing there would be a teaching spot for me after resignations and retirements. Instead, I walked away, never intending to return to education. Over a soul-searching year, I realized that education was where I was meant to be, and it called me back.

After completing my 30th year in education, my former students have become parents, authors, teachers, entrepreneurs, and community leaders. For several, I am still their mentor. I understand the impact of education and how it strengthens an entire community. I see how this work prepares the next generation to build upon and improve our society. I know the impact of education beyond the individual students. I realize what it will mean for the family they do not yet have, the children they will one day raise, and the community they will eventually lead. Education impacts all of it. Upon the shoulders of the education industry rests the hope for the future of our entire society. I consider myself beyond fortunate to be in a position to influence those hopes in an objective and meaningful way. It is the legacy we leave behind. It is what we owe for the very privilege of being alive. That is why I come back each year now.

Joel: Whenever the school year draws to a close, I ask myself, "What will bring me back next year?" The answer to that question is simple: the students. I understand that not all students are the same and that some can be more challenging than others. However, being able to make a real difference in a student's life is what keeps me going. Whether it is helping a student learn their timetable or teaching them the basic rules of chess, I find making any sort of difference worth it in the end. Earlier this year, after we had a second math diagnostic, one of my student's scores improved dramatically. He told me he knew who to thank for his gains and, when I asked who, he pointed at me. That makes it worth it.

Michael: I know I might sound crazy, but I still believe that one day students will be judged by the content of their character and not the color of their skin. Until that day, I vow to keep showing up. I still believe that all students deserve the right to a quality education and, until that day, I vow to keep showing up. I believe that students in inner-city schools should not be surprised by a Black male teacher or a Black principal, especially when most of the students are Black. So, until that day comes, I vow to keep showing up. I long for the day when students who represent the minority in a school population will not make up the majority of office referrals or individualized education plans. Until that day, I vow to keep showing up. I continue returning to the profession because I know and believe there is still work to be done. I hope that my position as a Black male educator will no longer be an anomaly, but the new norm resulting from policy changes and additional resources. Then, collectively, we can continue working to combat systems of inequity and racism that oppress and marginalize students of color all in the name of education. I continue to accept the call to be the educator and role model to my students and their families in the same way that my mentor, Mr. Biggs, was to me.

Steven: I enjoy serving. It really is that simple for me because educating children is meaningful work. Knowing that I am making a difference year after year is what keeps me going. I live in the community where I teach, and my children attend school in the same district. I believe that in order to change something, you must be a part of the solution. I live in the community with the students I serve, so that I can facilitate the change that I want to see. Whenever I am in the neighborhood or at the stores with my children, they always tease me because students are always yelling, "Hi, Mr. Mills!" and running over to give me hugs. I love that I can positively impact the next generation.

Summary

Most of the authors return to the profession each year because of the difference they are making in students' lives. There is also recognition that their impact extends beyond students by changing families, communities, and future generations. Some authors noted that they continue returning each year because there is more work to be done. Others expressed how deeply personal this work is for them. Authors David and Jay share that their service as educators is a part of God's purpose for their lives.

Chapter 10 Reflection

Record your thoughts, notes, and takeaways below.

_____

_____

_____

_____

_____

_____

_____

_____

_____

_____

_____

_____

_____

Black male educators are...

Indispensable

Essential

Necessary

Purposeful

Required

Life-changing

Powerful

Quintessential

Heroes

Contributing Author Biographies

David André Bennett holds a Bachelor of Music Education from The Ohio State University, a Master of Music in Choral Conducting Performance from Illinois State University, and a Master of Science in Educational Leadership from the University of Dayton. He is currently pursuing a doctorate from Concordia University Chicago and was recently inducted into the National Society of Leadership and Success. He holds professional memberships in the Association for Supervision and Curriculum Development, Ohio Association of Elementary School Administrators, Music Educators National Conference, and American Choral Directors Association. He is a former board member of the National Association for the Study and Performance of African American Music. He is married to lyric soprano, Dr. Dione Parker Bennett, and they have two beautiful daughters, Andréa Kaechele and Alexandria Leigh. He is the proudest Pawpaw to Josiah David and Micah Jahmir. Under David's leadership, his school was certified and named a *Leader in Me Lighthouse School* by FranklinCovey Education.

Ernest Clinkscale has been an educator for over 25 years. He was born in Youngstown, Ohio, and he graduated from Youngstown South in 1992. Ernest has always been committed to education as his father, Harold, and his mother, Carol, instilled that in him from an early age. He followed in his sister Angelique's footsteps and graduated from Ohio University. He has served as a classroom teacher, math coordinator, math supervisor, assistant principal, and head principal in numerous schools in central Ohio. He has been married to his wife, Nicole, who is also an educator, for 25 years. They have a daughter, Elissa, who is the absolute apple of her father's eye. Ernest and his family live in Columbus, Ohio.

Joel Vincent Coppadge II is a math educator in Delaware specializing in Pre-Algebra, Algebra I, and Geometry. With over six years of education experience, Joel successfully transitioned from paraprofessional to certified teacher. Each day, he demonstrates both the critical and fun aspects of mathematics to his students in the intermediate and middle school settings. Having earned a B.A. in mathematics from Morehouse College, an M.S. in applied mathematics from North Carolina A&T State University, and an M.A. in mathematics from Indiana University Bloomington, Joel recently completed the Alternative Route to Teacher Certification for secondary math at the University of Delaware. Outside of the classroom, Joel enjoys chess and empowers his community by teaching youth about hard work, discipline, and martial arts as a karate instructor.

Fredrick King, born and raised in Columbus, Indiana, received his bachelor's degree in psychology in 2013, with minors in counseling and Spanish from Ball State University. After providing mental health services to marginalized and foster care youth for two years, he continued his education at Indiana University Bloomington, where he obtained a master's degree in learning sciences, and an education specialist degree in school psychology in 2018. Fredrick worked as a school psychologist in northern Virginia supporting students in primary and secondary school settings. During this time, Fredrick has worked to develop equitable practices to increase achievement for marginalized students, including students of color and English Language Learners.

Jay Manning believes in Jesus Christ as his Lord and Savior. He loves all people regardless of race, religion, gender, or socioeconomic status. He is a mentor, educator, encourager, administrator, contributing author, son, friend, brother, coach, youth leader, and the Founder/CEO of Purpose Training LLC. Jay is a purpose-driven individual who loves the opportunity to help others reach their goals and full potential. Jay earned a bachelor's degree from Point University and a master's degree in education from Columbus State University. As a current high school assistant principal, Jay believes that every student has a unique purpose and he pushes students to be the best they can be in the classroom, in the community, and in life.

Steven D. Mills is a Cleveland, Ohio, native who graduated from Shaw High School. He serves as an elementary school principal in a suburban city near Dayton, Ohio. Steven earned a bachelor's degree in early childhood education from Central State University in Wilberforce, Ohio, and a master's degree in educational leadership from Miami University in Oxford, Ohio. Steven began his educational career as a kindergarten teacher but has also taught second grade and served as a literacy coach. Steven is a proud husband to his wife of 19 years, father of three biological children, four bonus children, and a father figure and mentor to many.

Scott Reeves has an illustrious career in education that has touched four different decades and two different centuries. A proud Ohio State alum, over the course of his 30-year career, he has been a teacher, varsity basketball coach, assistant principal, high school principal, and district-level administrator. He is currently an assistant superintendent in one of Ohio's largest school districts. His various roles have allowed him to be associated with several central Ohio community organizations. Reeves has served on the boards of a local food pantry as well as his state's athletic association. He has also held leadership positions in several community organizations. The Columbus, Ohio, native has been a presenter on various topics relating to education at both the state and national level. Scott Reeves and his wife, Valarie, have three children. They also love sports, traveling, and making a difference.

Tyler Rutledge has held a variety of roles before becoming a teacher. He brings numerous life experiences into the classroom to engage and connect with his students. This ranges from his time in the military to his time spent nursing. He has a son who is his world and one of his driving motivations throughout life and what he strives to do within education. Tyler is an avid traveler and animal lover who has a rabbit, two dogs, lizards, and fish. For his undergraduate degree, Tyler attended The Ohio State University earning a bachelor's degree in integrated science education. He obtained a master's degree in diversity and equity in education from the University of Illinois. Tyler's mission is to provide insights to his colleagues, school, and district as it relates to equitable practices for all students.

Michael J. Warren, Ed.D., a Pittsburgh native, graduated with a Bachelor of Science in Music Education (2017), a Master of Science in Education Administration (2018), and a Doctor of Education degree in Educational Leadership. As a scholar, Dr. Warren has been selected as a Project Hope Fellow (2020), a UCEA Barbara Jackson Scholar (2020-2022), a Clark Scholar for the American Educational Research Association (2022), the recipient of the Young, Gifted and Black Award (2020), the Duquesne Duke of the Decade recipient (2020), a Digital Promise Teacher of Color Advisory Council member (2019-2020), and finally, the awardee of the Dr. James E. Henderson Award (2020). Currently, Dr. Warren serves as a principal in central Ohio. Whether through music, teaching, or speaking events, he hopes to have an impact on many lives. Dr. Warren believes that when stakeholders work together, they can change the world.

Foreword Writer Biography

Michael R. Bean Jr., Ph.D., was a student-athlete at Hampton University and graduated with a Bachelor of Science degree in History. He went on to obtain a master's degree in educational leadership from Nova Southeastern University. While obtaining his master's degree he taught middle school History in northeastern Florida. Because he wanted to touch the lives of both students and families and engage the community, Bean began pursuing his Ph.D. in Educational Administration at Capella University. His primary goal was to study methods that would improve schools. Dr. Bean was able to put his learning into practice by serving as an administrator in the school system. Dr. Bean believes that all students are capable of learning regardless of their circumstances. He has been awarded several accolades that support this belief. Currently, Dr. Bean is an Associate Professor in the Educational Leadership and Administration program, Director of Diversity, Equity, and Inclusion, and Assistant Women's Basketball Coach at Concord University. In addition to these roles, Dr. Bean is the CEO of GSConsulting and author of *The Teaching Playbook*.

Book Compiler Biography

Garrett M. Carter, Ph.D., is a best-selling author and award-winning educator with a passion for developing tomorrow's leaders. With over a decade of experience in education, Garrett has been a teacher and leader in both K-12 and higher education settings. Having earned a B.S. and M.Ed. from the University of Cincinnati, Garrett completed his Ph.D. in Education Policy Studies at Indiana University. He has been featured in numerous newspapers, podcasts, and publications including the *HuffPost*. Dr. Carter currently serves as a middle school principal in central Ohio, where he lives with his wife and daughter.

Made in United States
Orlando, FL
17 October 2024